BIG-TIME RECORDS

SOCCER RECORDS

Published by Capstone Press, an imprint of Capstone.
1710 Roe Crest Drive
North Mankato, Minnesota 56003
capstonepub.com

SPORTS ILLUSTRATED KIDS is a trademark of ABG-SI LLC. Used with permission.

Library of Congress Cataloging-in-Publication Data
Names: Berglund, Bruce R., author.
Title: Big-time soccer records / by Bruce Berglund.
Description: North Mankato, Minnesota : Capstone Press, 2022. | Series: Sports illustrated kids big-time records | Includes bibliographical references and index. | Audience: Ages 8–11 | Audience: Grades 4–6
Identifiers: LCCN 2021004169 (print) | LCCN 2021004170 (ebook) | ISBN 9781496695482 (hardcover) | ISBN 9781977159090 (paperback) | ISBN 9781977159069 (ebook PDF)
Subjects: LCSH: Soccer—Records—Juvenile literature.
Classification: LCC GV943.4 .B47 2022 (print) | LCC GV943.4 (ebook) | DDC 796.334—dc23
LC record available at https://lccn.loc.gov/2021004169
LC ebook record available at https://lccn.loc.gov/2021004170

Summary: Nothing thrills soccer fans more than a ball sailing by the goalie's outstretched hands for the game-winning score—except when that big play sets a new record! From mind-boggling goals to the greatest fingertip saves, discover the greatest record-setting moments in soccer history.

Editorial Credits
Editor, Aaron Sautter; Designer, Bobbie Nuytten; Media Researcher, Morgan Walters; Production Specialist, Laura Manthe

Image Credits
Alamy: PA Images, 17; Associated Press: Mo Khursheed/TFV Media, 45; Getty Images: Clive Brunskill, 9, Daniela Porcelli, 36, Etsuo Hara, 23, FRANCK FIFE, 19, Ira L. Black - Corbis, 35, LLUIS GENE, 31; Newscom: Abaca Press/Niviere David, 49, Action Plus/Ulrik Pedersen, Cover, Charles Baus/Cal Sport Media, middle right 33, Jose Caballero/Digital press, 27, Kevin Langley/Cal Sport Media, 40, Maria Lysaker/Cal Sport Media, bottom right 33, Maurizio Borsari/www.aicfoto, 50, Panoramic/Juan Karita/Pool, 48, Panoramic/ ZUMA Press, top 47, picture-alliance/dpa, 7, THOMAS PETER/REUTERS, bottom right 47; Shutterstock: A.RICARDO, 56, charnsitr, 59, cristiano barni, bottom left 54, fifg, 8, grebeshkovmaxim, bottom 53, Jamie Lamor Thompson, 43, Keeton Gale, 37, marchello74, 16, Marco Iacobucci Epp, 5, Mikolaj Barbanell, 11, Photo Works, top right 33, bottom left 33, pingebat, 41, Romain Biard, 10, Stefan Ugljevarevic, bottom left 55, Ververidis Vasilis, 25; Sports Illustrated: Bob Martin, 21, Erick W. Rasco, bottom right 55, Jerry Cooke, 51, Peter Read Miller, 15, 39, top 53, Simon Bruty, 13, 29, bottom right 54

All records and statistics in this book are current through the 2020 season.

Printed and bound in the United States of America. PO4270

TABLE OF CONTENTS

WORDS IN **BOLD** APPEAR IN THE GLOSSARY.

THE WORLD'S MOST AMAZING GAME

On June 15, 2018, more than 40,000 people filled Saint Petersburg Stadium in St. Petersburg, Russia. Around the world, millions more people were watching on TV. Two great **rivals**, Spain and Portugal, faced off in the first round of the 2018 World Cup.

In the first half, Cristiano Ronaldo scored two goals to give Portugal the lead. But Spain pulled ahead 3–2 in the opening minutes of the second half.

As the game entered its final minutes Portugal pressed into Spain's end, trying to get the **equalizer**. Then Ronaldo was brought down outside the box. He set up for a free kick from 25 yards out. The ball curved around the wall of defenders and bent into the upper corner of the net. Portugal earned a draw in a spectacular opening match.

There was something even more special about Ronaldo's goal. At age 33, he was the oldest player to ever score a hat trick in a World Cup match. While celebrating, he rubbed his chin—like he had an old man's beard.

Cristiano Ronaldo scored a total of four goals in the first two matches of the 2018 World Cup.

Soccer has often been called "the beautiful game." When a player bends a free kick into the net or sends a 45-yard pass to the foot of her teammate, it is beautiful to watch.

Soccer is also called "the world's game." It is the most popular game in the world. More people around the globe play and watch soccer than any other sport.

Known in much of the world as football, soccer is an amazing sport. Some of the world's greatest athletes play soccer, such as Lionel Messi and Megan Rapinoe. Over the years, some players have become soccer legends by setting incredible records. Some records may never be broken, but soccer fans keep watching their favorite players to see if they can make history.

The Legendary Pelé

The youngest player ever to score a hat trick in the World Cup **tournament** was the amazing Pelé. In 1958, Pelé was only 17 years old when he played for Brazil. In the semifinal game against France, he scored three goals, all in the second half, and helped his team advance to the championship. In the final game, he scored twice more to help Brazil win its first World Cup championship.

Brazilian striker Pelé is a soccer legend.

Chapter One

BIG-TIME WORLD CUP RECORDS

Most Men's World Cup Championships

Since 1930, the world's best men's teams have competed every four years in the World Cup competition.

When a national team wins the World Cup title, it earns the right to wear a star on its jersey. The men's team with the most stars on its shirt is Brazil. Above the Brazilian **crest** are five stars, one for each of the country's World Cup wins.

Winners of FIFA Men's World Cup

TEAM	YEARS
Brazil	1958, 1962, 1970, 1994, 2002
Germany	1954, 1974, 1990, 2014
Italy	1934, 1938, 1982, 2006
Argentina	1978, 1986
France	1998, 2018
Uruguay	1930, 1950
England	1966
Spain	2010

Brazil had two of the best players in the world when it won the 2002 World Cup: striker Ronaldo (left) and midfielder Ronaldinho (right).

Soccer is the national game of Brazil. When the national team wins, people across the country celebrate. When the team loses, there is nationwide sadness. Brazil is always competitive. Every year, the team is near the top of the world rankings in men's soccer. As the saying goes: The English invented soccer, but the Brazilians perfected it.

Most Women's World Cup Championships

The Women's World Cup began in 1991. The tournament has now been held eight times. Of those tournaments, the U.S. Women's National Team (USWNT) has won the championship 4 times. No other women's national team has won it more.

The U.S. team's dominance in women's soccer is no surprise. The United States has more girls and women playing soccer than any other country. In fact, almost half of all female soccer players in the world live in America. With so many girls and women playing the sport, the talent level is very high. The USWNT is made up of the very best players in the country.

However, other countries are beginning to catch up. In other parts of the world, more and more girls join soccer teams every year.

USWNT co-captain Alex Morgan scored five goals in the opening game of the 2019 Women's World Cup.

USWNT veteran Megan Rapinoe scored three goals to help win the 2019 Women's World Cup.

FIFA Women's World Cup, Champions and Runners-Up

YEAR	CHAMPION	RUNNER-UP	HOST COUNTRY
1991	USA	Norway	China
1995	Norway	Germany	Sweden
1999	USA	China	USA
2003	Germany	Sweden	USA
2007	Germany	Brazil	China
2011	Japan	USA	Germany
2015	USA	Japan	Canada
2019	USA	Netherlands	France

The World Cup's Greatest Scorers

Germany's Miroslav Klose was 24 years old when he scored his first World Cup goal at the 2002 tournament—on a **header**. He scored his second World Cup goal just 5 minutes later—also on a header. In Germany, he was already famous for his goal-scoring celebration. He did a front flip like a gymnast.

Klose played in four World Cup tournaments. His team won the tournament in 2014. In that tournament, Klose scored his 16th World Cup goal in Germany's semifinal win over Brazil. He'd just broken the record for most all-time goals in the Men's World Cup.

Brazilian forward Marta is the top scorer in the Women's World Cup. Marta has scored 17 goals in 5 tournaments. She is the only player in the world to score in that many tournaments.

Marta is regarded as the greatest women's soccer player of all time—and she's still playing. The next Women's World Cup will be played in 2023. Marta will be 37 years old, one year older than Miroslav Klose when he scored his last goal. She has a great chance to add to her record.

Most Women's World Cup Goals

PLAYER	COUNTRY	TOTAL GOALS
Marta	Brazil	17
Birgit Prinz	Germany	14
Abby Wambach	USA	14
Michelle Akers	USA	12

Most Men's World Cup Goals

PLAYER	COUNTRY	TOTAL GOALS
Miroslav Klose	Germany	16
Ronaldo	Brazil	15
Gerd Müller	Germany	14
Just Fontaine	France	13
Pelé	Brazil	12

Marta helped Brazil win silver at the 2008 Olympic Games.

Largest Crowd for Women's World Cup Match

On July 10, 1999, the women's national teams of China and the United States met at the Rose Bowl in California. Their match would decide the winner of the Women's World Cup.

The teams battled for a full 90 minutes in temperatures of more than 100 degrees Fahrenheit (38 degrees Celsius). But neither side could score a goal. After another 30 minutes of extra time, the two teams were still deadlocked at 0–0. Exhausted by the heat, players on each team prepared for a **shootout** to decide the winner. Each team would have five chances to score. The team with the most goals would win. Who would be the champion?

It came down to the final kick. "I just stepped up and hit it," said Brandi Chastain. The stadium erupted in cheers. 90,185 people in the stands witnessed the U.S. Women's National Team lift the trophy after Chastain's kick. It was the largest crowd ever for a Women's World Cup match or any women's soccer match.

Meeting the President

After their amazing win in the World Cup final, the USWNT was on the cover of magazines and went on TV talk shows. They also went to the White House and met U.S. President Bill Clinton, who had been in the crowd at the Rose Bowl.

The U.S. Women's National Team celebrated together after winning the 1999 Women's World Cup.

Largest Crowd at a Men's World Cup Match

In 1950 Brazil hosted the Men's World Cup. The whole country expected their national team to win the tournament.

Brazilians were very confident about their team's chances. The Brazilian government even built a new stadium in Rio de Janeiro for the championship game. The stadium was called the Maracanã.

Brazil's national team made it to the final game. The Maracanã was filled with more people than it could hold. Guards didn't even check tickets. They let everybody in. The stadium's **capacity** was 155,000 people. But on July 16, 1950, more than 200,000 people came to see Brazil win the championship. It was the largest crowd ever to watch a soccer game.

However, Brazil fans left disappointed. Uruguay defeated Brazil 2–1. The deciding goal in the 79th minute silenced the huge crowd. Even to this today, the stunning loss at the Maracanã haunts Brazilian fans.

The Maracanã hosted the final game of the 2014 World Cup. The stadium has been redesigned, so it now holds 78,838 people.

They Shocked the World

The 1950 World Cup was the scene of one of the most amazing upsets in soccer history. The English team was one of the best in the world. Its players were **professionals**. At the time, soccer wasn't very popular in the United States. The U.S. players were not pros. They instead worked as teachers and postal carriers. But in the group stage of the tournament, they shocked the soccer world. The U.S. team beat England 1–0. Today the U.S. men's and women's teams honor the 1950 team in some games. They wear the same style of jersey—white with a single red stripe.

Chapter Two

BIG-TIME CHAMPIONS LEAGUE RECORDS

Each year, soccer clubs across Europe hope to compete in the Champions League, which is organized by the Union of European Football Associations (UEFA). A few clubs represent tiny countries like Montenegro and Andorra. Stronger leagues in bigger countries send their top two or three teams. The very best leagues—the English Premier League, the Spanish La Liga, Italy's Serie A, and the German Bundesliga—have their top four teams in the Champions League.

The team with the most Champions League titles comes from Spain. Real Madrid won the first tournament in 1956, and then set a record by winning five years in a row. Real Madrid has had another recent **dynasty**. Between 2014 and 2018, the team won four Champions League titles, including three in a row.

Most Champions League Titles

CLUB	TITLES
Real Madrid	13
AC Milan	7
Liverpool	6
Bayern Munich	6
Barcelona	5

Real Madrid's Luka Modric (left) and coach Zinedine Zidane (right) celebrated winning the 2018 UEFA Champions League match against Liverpool.

As a player with Real Madrid, Zinedine Zidane won the 2002 Champions League. After becoming the club's manager in 2016, Zidane led Real Madrid to three straight titles. Midfielder Luka Modric was one of the best players on those championship teams.

Most Champions League Goals

Cristiano Ronaldo scored his first goal in the Champions League in 2007. He was just 22 years old and a member of Manchester United.

Cristiano Ronaldo has won five Champions League titles so far. His first title came with Man U. He earned his other four titles with Real Madrid. Ronaldo joined Juventus in 2018. If he wins another title with his new club, he'll tie two different records. He will tie Francisco Gento for six total titles. And he will tie Clarence Seedorf, who is the only player to win titles with three different clubs.

But Ronaldo stands alone as the Champions League top goal scorer. Through 2020, he had scored 134 goals in the tournament, ahead of Lionel Messi's 119 goals. They are the only two players to score more than 100 Champions League goals in their careers.

Cristiano Ronaldo's Champions League Goals by Season

SEASON	NUMBER OF GOALS
2006–07	3
2007–08	8
2008–09	4
2009–10	7
2010–11	6
2011–12	10
2012–13	12
2013–14	17
2014–15	10
2015–16	16
2016–17	12
2017–18	15
2018–19	6
2019–20	4
2020–21	4

Cristiano Ronaldo won his first Champions League
title with Manchester United in 2008.

Most Penalty Kicks for a Champions League Title

Champions League finals have been decided by **penalty kick** shootouts 11 times. Most recently, Real Madrid won the 2016 title over Atlético Madrid in a shootout after finishing regular and extra time with the score tied. Cristiano Ronaldo scored the deciding penalty kick to take the trophy.

But there is one penalty kick that Ronaldo probably doesn't want to remember. In 2008, he played with Manchester United in the Champions League final against Chelsea. Deadlocked 1–1 after extra time, the teams went to a shootout. Each side traded goals in the first two rounds.

With the teams tied, it was Cristiano Ronaldo's turn. He approached the ball then stopped quickly, hoping to throw off Chelsea keeper Petr Cech. But the goalie didn't move. He knew that whenever Ronaldo approached a penalty kick and stopped, he kicked to the right. That's what Ronaldo did, and Petr Cech made the save.

Ronaldo's mistake didn't cost Manchester United the title. In the fifth round the teams were tied 4–4. Chelsea's John Terry could have won it but he hit the post with his kick. The two teams kept going in sudden death. The first to miss a shot would lose. In the sixth round both teams made their goals. Finally, in the seventh round, Man U goalie Edwin van der Sar stopped Nicolas Anelka's kick. A record fourteen players had taken kicks. The final tally was 6–5, giving United its third Champions League title.

Chelsea's John Terry (on ground) doubled over in disbelief after missing a game-winning shot against Manchester U at the 2008 UEFA Champions League final.

Chapter Three

BIG-TIME EUROPEAN LEAGUE RECORDS

Largest Attendance in Europe

Soccer is the most popular sport in Europe. Almost every country has its own league, and fans fill stadiums to support their favorite clubs. The largest stadium in Europe is the famous Camp Nou, home of FC Barcelona. When Barça plays in big games against their rivals, the stadium can hold nearly 100,000 enthusiastic fans, known as *Barcelonistas*.

Although Barcelona has the largest stadium, it doesn't have the highest average attendance. In fact, Spain's top league, La Liga, doesn't even draw the most fans. The European league with the record for highest average attendance is Germany's Bundesliga league. An average of 43,000 fans attend each match in the top German league.

The English Premier League (EPL) draws fewer average spectators for each match. But the EPL has more teams and more matches during the season. For this reason, the league draws the most total fans each year. In fact, more than 1 million more fans attend EPL matches than the Bundesliga.

Dortmund fans cheered during a 2015 UEFA Europa League match.

Borussia Dortmund has the highest attendance of any club in the Bundesliga league, and of any club in Europe.

European Soccer Clubs with Highest Average Attendance

Borussia Dortmund, Bundesliga: 80,230

Manchester United, EPL: 75,218

FC Barcelona, La Liga: 74,876

Bayern Munich, Bundesliga: 73,781

Real Madrid, La Liga: 69,822

Pro Sports Leagues with Highest Average Attendance

National Football League: 67,100

Bundesliga: 43,449

English Premier League: 38,168

Japan Professional Baseball: 30,928

Major League Baseball: 28,176

European Club with the Most Trophies

In the United States, pro sports leagues award only one trophy. Each season, there is only one champion in pro baseball, basketball, football, and hockey.

But things are different in European soccer. In each national league, one club wins the league title by finishing at the top of the standings. Most countries also have a cup tournament. These tournaments are open to nearly every club, from the top professionals to teams made up of part-time players. Some countries also have a match between the winners of the league title and the cup tournament. The winner gets yet another trophy.

Clubs also compete for international trophies. These include the Champions League or the FIFA Club World Cup that are awarded to the world's very best teams.

FC Barcelona has won the Spanish cup competition, the Copa del Rey, an amazing 30 times. The team has also won 26 league titles, five Champions League titles, three World Cup titles, and multiple wins in several other trophy competitions. In total, Barça has won 95 major trophies. And every season, they add more to their collection.

Most Major Competition Wins*

CLUB	LEAGUE TITLES	NATIONAL CUP TOURNAMENT	OTHER NATIONAL TROPHIES	
FC Barcelona	26	30	19	
Real Madrid	34	19	13	
Bayern Munich	30	20	14	
Juventus	36	13	9	
Manchester United	20	12	26	
Liverpool	19	7	25	

FC Barcelona has won more trophies than any other club in Europe.

EUROPEAN TROPHIES	WORLD TROPHIES	TOTAL
17	3	95
19	7	92
9	4	77
9	2	69
6	2	66
13	1	65

*Stats listed are through the 2019–20 season.

This ranking of trophy winners is from the top European leagues—EPL, La Liga, Serie A, and Bundesliga. In smaller countries, often only one or two clubs win almost all of the trophies. In Scotland, one of two clubs, Rangers or Celtic, have won the league almost every year.

Most Goals in a Season

Lionel Messi was just 6 years old when he joined a youth soccer team in his hometown of Rosario, Argentina. By the age of 12, he had scored an astounding 500 goals.

Messi wanted to be a professional soccer player. In 2000, at just 13 years old, Messi had a tryout with FC Barcelona. The club's manager saw great potential, but there was a problem. Because of a problem with his growth **hormones**, Messi was a very small player. He would be too small to play pro soccer unless he had special medical treatment, which was too expensive for his family.

But Barcelona decided to take a chance. They offered Messi a contract, and the club agreed to pay for his medical treatment. Messi and his family moved to Barcelona, where he joined the club's youth academy.

Barcelona's gamble paid off in a big way. Since Messi became a starter for the club in 2003, Barcelona has won 35 trophies. He holds the record for most goals in the history of La Liga.

Messi's most amazing record came in the 2011–12 season. In league games, cup matches, and the Champions League, he scored a combined total of 73 goals. There had never been a scoring performance like that in European soccer.

After living for so many years in Spain, Messi could have played for the Spanish national team. But he instead chose to play for his home country of Argentina. "I wanted to play for my national team because I love Argentina and these are the only colors I want to wear," he said.

Messi made his debut with Argentina's national team in 2005. He has become Argentina's top goal scorer, with 71 international goals in 142 games for the team.

Most Watched Rivalry in Europe

World soccer seems to have a language of its own. For one thing, most people around the world call the sport *fútbol*, or football, which is much different than American football. There are other words unique to soccer too. One is "derby" (pronounced *dahr-bee*). This word describes a longstanding rivalry between two clubs.

Derbies in European football are some of the most-watched matches of the season. There is always a lot of excitement about a derby, even if both teams are down in the "table" (the soccer term used for league standings).

Other Popular Derbies in Europe

Some of the biggest derbies in European soccer are between clubs in the same city. Like *El Clasico*, these derbies also have interesting nicknames.

DERBY NAME	TEAMS	CITY	LEAGUE
The Old Firm	Celtic and Rangers	Glasgow, Scotland	Scottish Premier League
North London Derby	Arsenal and Tottenham	London, England	English Premier League
The Intercontinental Derby	Fenerbahçe and Galatasaray	Istanbul, Turkey	Turkish Super League
Derby of the Lighthouse	Genoa and Sampdoria	Genoa, Italy	Italian Serie A
Derby of the Eternal Enemies	Olympiacos and Panathinaikos	Athens, Greece	Greek Super League

The most watched derby in European football—one of the biggest rivalries in all of sports—is between Real Madrid and Barcelona. The two teams are almost always competing for the title in La Liga. And each year they are among the best teams competing in the Champions League. Their rivalry is called *El Clasico*, or The Classic.

El Clasico is a huge event, and not only in Spain. The soccer match is shown on television in 185 countries. More than 500 million people tune in each time the rival teams play each other.

Lionel Messi (center) in action during the 2019 *El Clasico* match.

Chapter Four

BIG-TIME NORTH AMERICAN RECORDS

Most Major League Soccer Titles

Major League Soccer (MLS) played its first season in 1996 with 10 teams. At the time, soccer wasn't very popular in the United States. MLS tried different things to increase interest for American sports fans. For example, the game clock at MLS games once counted down to 0:00, just like in football or basketball. But today the clock counts up instead.

Today, MLS has 26 teams across the U.S. and Canada. The league's most successful team is one of the original 10 in 1996—the Los Angeles Galaxy. The team won its first MLS Cup in 2002. The LA Galaxy has won five total MLS championships, more than any other team.

CLUB	LEAGUE TITLES	YEARS
LA Galaxy	5	2002, 2005, 2011, 2012, 2014
D.C. United	4	1996, 1997, 1999, 2004
Five teams tied with 2 titles.		

European and Latin American stars with LA Galaxy

The LA Galaxy is so named because, like a galaxy, Los Angeles is a city full of movie stars. The team has also brought stars of the soccer world to MLS.

DAVID BECKHAM, 2007–2012
David Beckham was the most famous soccer player in the world when he signed with the LA Galaxy.

ZLATAN IBRAHIMOVIC, 2018–2019
Zlatan scored two goals in his first action with the Galaxy, including a game-winning header in extra time.

ROBBIE KEANE, 2011–2016
Irish forward Robbie Keane led the Galaxy in scoring four years in a row.

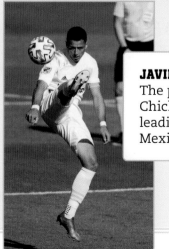

JAVIER HERNANDEZ, 2020–
The player known as Chicharito is the all-time leading scorer for the Mexican national team.

Most Goals in an MLS Season

Two of the newest teams in MLS feature two of the best young scorers in the league. One set the record for most goals in a season in 2018. The other broke the record the very next season.

Venezuelan striker Josef Martinez joined Atlanta United in 2017. He started off hot, scoring five goals in his first three games. He finished the season with 19 goals in just 17 starts. The next year Martinez just kept scoring. He scored 28 goals in 26 matches to break the single-season record. He added three more to finish the season with an incredible 31 goals.

But Martinez's record lasted only one season. Mexican winger Carlos Vela became a star for Los Angeles FC right away in 2018, the team's first season in MLS. In 2019 he scored 20 goals in his first 21 games, the fastest any MLS player had reached that milestone. He kept scoring goals, and in the final game of the season, Vela smashed Martinez's record with a hat trick. He finished the season with 34 goals and the league's Most Valuable Player (MVP) award.

These two young players broke the scoring record two seasons in a row. Only time will tell how many times Vela and Martinez might break their own scoring records.

Atlanta United's Josef Martinez seemed to float in the air to perform a stunning bicycle kick in a 2019 match against Philadelphia Union.

Top Scorer in National Women's Soccer League

The best female players from the U.S. and Canada play pro soccer in the National Women's Soccer League. There are ten teams in the NWSL. Portland Thorns FC and North Carolina Courage have been the two most successful teams. Each team has won the NWSL championship twice.

The members of the U.S. Women's National Team play for different clubs in the NWSL. But the all-time scoring leader in league history doesn't play for Team USA. Instead, Samantha Kerr is captain of the Australian national team. In seven seasons in the NWSL, Sam Kerr scored an amazing 78 goals. In 2017 she played for Sky Blue FC. In a game against Seattle Reign FC, her team was down 3–0 at halftime. Kerr scored a single-game record of four goals in the second half and led her team to a win.

Chicago Red Stars player Samantha Kerr (#20) takes a shot at the goal during a 2019 match against North Carolina Courage.

The Portland Thorns are one of the winningest teams in the NWSL. They also have one of the strongest fan communities. In 2019 the team set an attendance record when 25,218 fans watched the Thorns defeat the North Carolina Courage.

Most NCAA Women's Soccer Titles

One of the most successful teams in any sport, women's or men's, is the University of North Carolina women's soccer team. The Tar Heels have won 21 national championships. The next teams on the list aren't even close. Stanford and Notre Dame have each won three titles.

How did North Carolina's team become so dominant? First, they've had many incredible players over the years. During superstar Mia Hamm's four years with the team, the Tar Heels won 94 games and lost only once. Hamm and her teammates led North Carolina to four NCAA titles.

Mia Hamm played on the U.S. Women's National Team from 1987 to 2004. When she retired, she had the record for most goals scored by anyone in international competition. Today, Mia Hamm is co-owner of Los Angeles FC in MLS and is on the board of directors for the Italian men's team, AS Roma.

Greatest Teams Ever: Teams with 9 Consecutive Championships

TEAM	SPORT/LEAGUE	CONSECUTIVE CHAMPIONSHIPS
Juventus	Soccer/Italian Serie A	2011–2020
University of North Carolina Tar Heels	Soccer/NCAA Division I	1986–1994
Rangers FC	Soccer/Scottish Football League	1988–1997
Celtic FC	Soccer/Scottish Football League	1965–1974
Celtic FC	Soccer/Scottish premier League	2011–2020
Tokyo Giants	Professional Baseball/Japan	1965–1973
University of Iowa Hawkeyes	Men's wrestling/ NCAA Division I	1978–1986
Soviet National Hockey Team	Men's hockey/world championships and Olympics	1963–1971

Mia Hamm made her mark as a star player for UNC Tar Heels before becoming a team leader for the U.S. Women's National Team.

Most Gold Cup Titles

Every four years, the World Cup tournament is held to determine the world's best national soccer team. Between World Cup years, continental tournaments decide which teams are best in specific areas of the globe.

The U.S. Men's National Team competes in the Gold Cup. The tournament is held every two years. Matches are often held at stadiums in the United States. The title match of the 2019 Gold Cup was held at Soldier Field, home of the NFL's Chicago Bears.

The U.S. men's team has won the Gold Cup six times. But another team has won the trophy even more. Mexico holds the record with eight Gold Cup championships. Mexico and the USA have played each other six times in the final game of the tournament. Mexico has won five of those championship matches.

The Mexican national team celebrated after defeating the United States 1–0 in the 2019 Gold Cup.

In men's soccer, there are six continental championships. These include the Asian Cup; the African Cup of Nations; the European Championship; the OFC Nations Cup for countries in Oceania like New Zealand and Tahiti; the Copa América for South America; and the Gold Cup for North America and the Caribbean.

Most Championships in Continental Tournaments

TOURNAMENT	COUNTRY	CHAMPIONSHIPS
African Cup of Nations	Egypt	7
Asian Cup	Japan	4
Copa América	Uruguay	15
European Championship	Germany and Spain	tie, 3 each
Gold Cup	Mexico	8
OFC Nations Cup	New Zealand	5

Largest Crowds in MLS

When Major League Soccer began in the 1990s, soccer wasn't as popular in America as it is now. Crowds at stadiums were pretty small. But today MLS draws millions of fans. Teams like the Seattle Sounders, Minnesota United, Los Angeles FC, and Sporting Kansas City draw large crowds of fans every year.

One team has all the records for MLS attendance. Atlanta United FC joined the league in 2017. The team immediately started drawing huge crowds to Mercedes-Benz Stadium, the arena they share with the Atlanta Falcons. In its first season, Atlanta United set records for most fans at an MLS game and had the highest average attendance.

The team has continued to be popular and has even broken its own records. On December 8, 2018, Atlanta United beat the Portland Timbers for the MLS Cup. More than 73,000 people filled the stadium. Not only does Atlanta United have the largest crowds in MLS, but its average attendance is also the 10th highest of any soccer team in the world.

Biggest Soccer Crowds in the United States

EVENT	TEAMS	DATE	STADIUM	ATTENDANCE
2014 International Champions Cup	Manchester United vs. Real Madrid	August 2, 2014	Michigan Stadium	109,318
2016 International Champions Cup	Real Madrid vs. Chelsea	July 30, 2016	Michigan Stadium	105,826
1984 Olympics	France vs. Brazil	August 11, 1984	Rose Bowl	101,799
2018 International Champions Cup	Manchester United vs. Liverpool	July 28, 2018	Michigan Stadium	101,254
1984 Olympics	Yugoslavia vs. Italy	August 10, 1984	Rose Bowl	100,374

Mercedes-Benz Stadium

Mercedes-Benz Stadium in Atlanta, Georgia, is home to both Atlanta United FC and the Atlanta Falcons football team. It opened in 2017 and can seat more than 70,000 fans.

Highest Average MLS Attendance, 2019

TEAMS	AVERAGE ATTENDANCE
Atlanta United FC	52,510
Seattle Sounders	40,247
FC Cincinnati	27,336
Portland Timbers	25,218
Toronto FC	25,048

Largest TV Audience in the United States

U.S. soccer fans now fill stadiums across the country. Millions more watch matches on TV. Each year, the Champions League final draws more than 3 million TV viewers in the United States. Big matches between clubs in the Mexican League are watched by more than 2 million people.

The biggest soccer events on TV are always the World Cup tournaments. Even though the U.S. Men's National Team did not qualify for the 2018 World Cup, many American soccer fans still watched the matches. Nearly 12 million people watched the World Cup final between France and Croatia.

2015 Largest U.S. TV Audiences for Major Sports Events

The U.S. TV audience for the 2015 Women's World Cup was larger than any pro sports event, except the Super Bowl. In 2015 more than 114 million people watched the Super Bowl on TV.

New England Patriots vs. Seattle Seahawks, Super Bowl XLIX
114.4 million viewers

USA vs. Japan, Women's World Cup Final
26.7 million viewers

Golden State Warriors vs. Cleveland Cavaliers, Final game, 2015 NBA Finals,
23.3 million viewers

Kansas City Royals vs. New York Mets, 2015 World Series Game 5,
17.2 million viewers

Chicago Blackhawks vs. Tampa Bay Lightning, 2015 Stanley Cup Finals Game 6,
8 million viewers

But 12 million people is still much smaller than the largest American audience to ever watch a game on TV. In 2015, 26.7 million people watched the final of the Women's World Cup. The U.S. women's team faced Japan, four years after Japan had won the World Cup in a penalty shootout. The U.S. team ended up taking home the trophy, as well as the record for the biggest TV audience for a soccer game.

The U.S. Women's National Team celebrated winning the Women's World Cup in 2015.

SOCCER'S GREATEST SCORING RECORDS

Most International Goals

Christine Sinclair was just 16 years old when she scored her first goal for the Canadian national women's team. Twenty years later, on January 29, 2020, she scored her 185th goal to break the record for most goals in international soccer.

The previous record had been set by Abby Wambach, who had played for the USWNT. Wambach quickly congratulated Sinclair for her achievement. In an online message she wrote, "Christine: History is made. Your victory is our victory. We celebrate with you."

Sinclair's record-setting match also marked her 290th cap for Canada. When a soccer player plays in a match for her or his national team, the player is said to "earn a cap," or that they were "capped." A hundred years ago, athletes received an actual cap whenever they played for their national team. Christine Sinclair is now the most-capped active soccer player in the world. But she'll have to play a lot more games before she can claim the all-time record. That record is held by American Kristine Lilly, who was capped 354 times during her career.

Christine Sinclair (center) has been nominated for FIFA Women's Player of the Year several times.

The Perfect Score

Abby Wambach scored 184 goals in her international career. Her most amazing goal came against Brazil in the semifinals of the 2011 Women's World Cup. The U.S. women's team was down by one goal in extra time. Then, with time running down, Megan Rapinoe kicked a 45-yard (41-m) cross pass into the box in front of the goal. Abby Wambach was ready for it. She timed it perfectly, jumped up, and put an incredible header into the corner of the net. The goal was voted the greatest moment ever in Women's World Cup history.

Abby Wambach celebrated after netting a header against Brazil in the 2011 Women's World Cup.

Soccer fans today are lucky. They are treated to two of the most amazing players in the sport's history. For 10 years between 2008 and 2017, nobody other than Lionel Messi or Cristiano Ronaldo won the Ballon d'Or (the Golden Ball). It is the most prestigious award for the world's top soccer player.

LIONEL MESSI*

Born: June 24, 1987

First pro match (FC Barcelona):
November 16, 2003

First cap (Argentina):
August 17, 2005

Ballon d'Or Awards: 2009, 2010, 2011, 2012, 2015, 2019

International goals: 71

Club goals: 634

Average goals per game: .81

League titles: 10

Champions League titles: 4

Goals in Champions League games: 115

Goals in World Cup games: 6

Hat tricks: 54

Olympic gold medal with Argentina, 2008

Record: most total goals scored in a year, 91 in 2012

Head to head with Ronaldo:
36 matches, 16 wins, 22 goals

*Stats listed are through the 2019–20 season.

Years from now, people will still be talking about Ronaldo and Messi as two of soccer's all-time greats. People will still be debating: Which one was better? Few soccer players in history can compare to their amazing achievements.

CRISTIANO RONALDO*

Born: February 5, 1985

First pro match (Sporting Lisbon): October 7, 2002

First cap (Portugal): August 20, 2003

Ballon d'Or Awards: 2008, 2013, 2014, 2016, 2017

International goals: 102

Club goals: 638

Average goals per game: .73

League titles: 7

Champions League titles: 5

Goals in Champions League games: 130

Goals in World Cup games: 7

Hat tricks: 56

European Championship with Portugal, 2016

Record: most international goals scored in a year, 32 in 2017

Head to head with Messi: 36 matches, 11 wins, 21 goals

*Stats listed are through the 2019–20 season.

The Greatest Scorer of All Time

Messi and Ronaldo will go down in history as two of soccer's most amazing players. But there is only one player who can be called the greatest.

His name is Edson Arantes do Nascimento. When he was in school his friends called him Pelé. It was just a made-up name, but it stuck.

Pelé grew up with a poor family in Brazil. But he didn't let that stop him from success. He loved soccer and knew he wanted to be a pro player. Pelé signed his first professional soccer contract in 1956 when he was only 15 years old. He scored a goal in his very first game. The next season, at age 16, he was the top scorer in the league.

Pelé's career lasted 21 amazing years. When he retired, he was one of the most famous athletes in the world and he owned many records. Since then, some of his records have been broken. But there is no question that Pelé is soccer's most amazing player.

Pelé (third from left) said in an interview that the current player he would have most liked to have as a teammate is Lionel Messi (second from left).

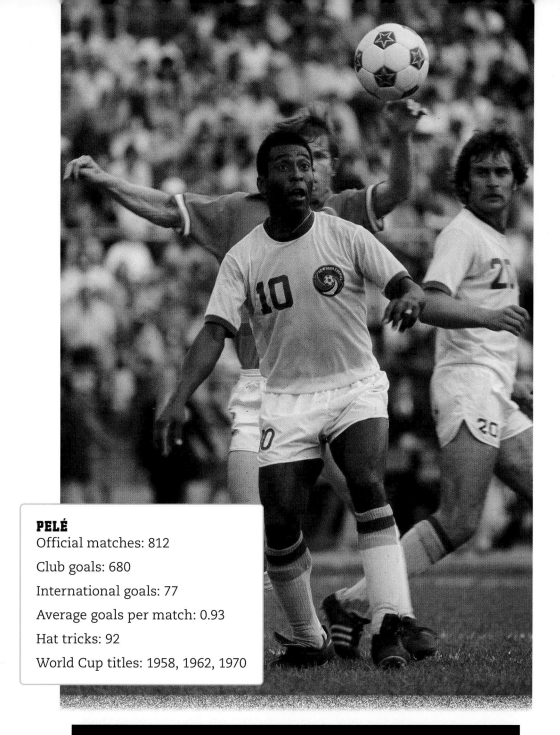

PELÉ

Official matches: 812

Club goals: 680

International goals: 77

Average goals per match: 0.93

Hat tricks: 92

World Cup titles: 1958, 1962, 1970

The *Guinness Book of World Records* says that Pelé scored 1,279 goals in 1,363 matches. But that total includes exhibition games. When Pelé became famous, his Brazilian club team, Santos FC, played many unofficial games so that more people could see the great player.

Chapter Six

THE MOST POPULAR GAME IN THE WORLD

Soccer's First $1 Billion Player

Soccer fans love to wear soccer shirts. Wearing a jersey lets fans show off their favorite team or player. Teams create new shirts every season, along with second or even third shirts in different colors. Fans are excited to get each season's new designs.

There are always a lot of cool-looking jerseys for fans to buy and add to their collections. Each year fans around the world spend billions of dollars on soccer jerseys. When Cristiano Ronaldo joined Juventus in 2018, the team sold $60 million worth of shirts in one day!

David Beckham jerseys were the most popular for the longest time. During the 11 seasons Beckham played for Manchester United, people all over the world wore red shirts with Beckham's name and number 7 on the back. Each time he joined a new club, fans bought the new shirt. In total, fans bought more than 10 million David Beckham shirts during his career. He was the first soccer player to sell more than $1 billion in shirts and shoes to fans.

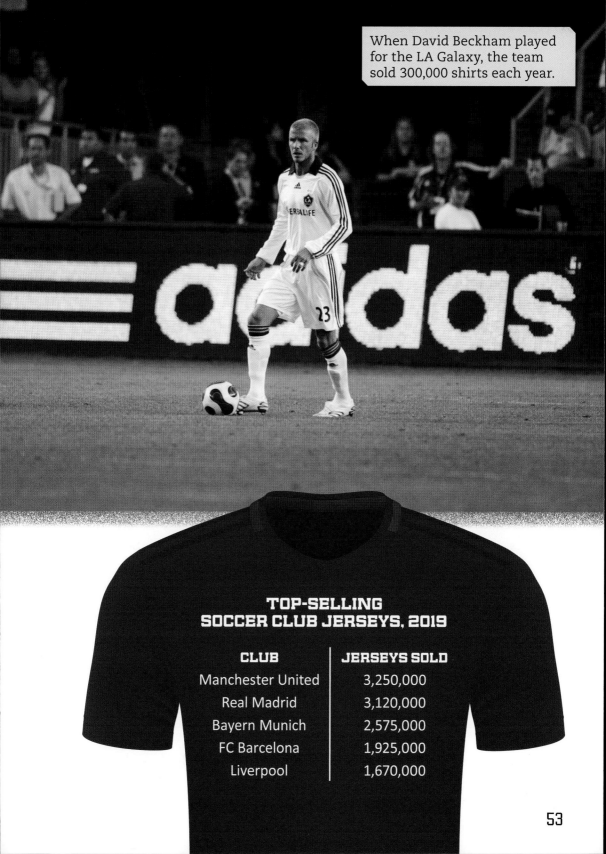

When David Beckham played for the LA Galaxy, the team sold 300,000 shirts each year.

TOP-SELLING SOCCER CLUB JERSEYS, 2019

CLUB	JERSEYS SOLD
Manchester United	3,250,000
Real Madrid	3,120,000
Bayern Munich	2,575,000
FC Barcelona	1,925,000
Liverpool	1,670,000

Most Followed Athlete in the World

Most pro athletes are active on social media. They use Twitter, Instagram, and Facebook to connect with fans. Some famous athletes show videos of their workouts, so fans can see how much work goes into playing pro sports. Some players post photos of their activity with charities to encourage fans to help out. Sometimes famous players post photos from home to show they are normal people who love their families.

Athletes with Most Followers on Social Media*

CRISTIANO RONALDO, 488 million followers

LIONEL MESSI, 298 million followers

Of the 100 most-followed athletes on social media, 63 are pro soccer players. The player with the largest following is Cristiano Ronaldo. He has more online followers than any other athlete by far. In 2019 fans liked, shared, and commented on Ronaldo's posts 1.7 billion times. That's nearly 1 billion more times than the next most popular athlete on the list, Lionel Messi.

NEYMAR, 274 million followers

LEBRON JAMES, 157 million followers

*Numbers listed include followers on Twitter, Facebook, and Instagram through March, 2021.

The Most–Watched Game

The World Cup is a worldwide event. Every four years, hundreds of millions of people on every continent tune in to watch the games.

The most-watched World Cup match of all time was the 2014 final between Germany and Argentina. The German team had just destroyed Brazil 7–1 in the semifinals, shocking Brazilian fans everywhere. Meanwhile, Argentina was led to the final by Lionel Messi, who was awarded the Golden Ball trophy as the best player in the tournament.

The German national team celebrated after winning the 2014 World Cup.

After playing 90 minutes without a goal, the two teams went into extra time. Germany took the lead in the 113th minute. Near the end of extra time, Messi had the chance to tie the score on a free kick. But his 30-yard (27-m) kick sailed over the crossbar. When time ran out, Germany was champion of the world.

The exciting final between a team from Europe and a team from South America set the record for largest TV audience in history. Over 1 billion people tuned in at some point during the game. At the time, the world's population was 7 billion. So, on July 13, 2014, more than 14% of the world's population was tuned in to watch a soccer game.

World's Most-Watched Sporting Events

2008 Beijing Summer Olympics,
Opening Ceremony,
2 billion viewers

2014 Men's World Cup,
Germany vs. Argentina,
1 billion viewers

2014 Champions League Final,
Real Madrid vs. Atletico Madrid,
380 million viewers

2017 Super Bowl LI,
New England Patriots vs. Atlanta Falcons,
172 million viewers

Best-Selling Sports Video Game

Do you like playing sports video games? Many people do, both kids and adults.

Just as soccer is the most popular sport in the world, it is also the most popular sports video game in the world. Since the first version was released in 1993, EA Sports *FIFA* has sold more than 325 million copies. That is more than twice as many copies as the next most popular sports game, *Madden NFL*.

FIFA is not just a fun video game. It's also been important in helping soccer to become a popular sport in the United States. As more and more people played *FIFA*, they learned about the world's best clubs and players. *FIFA* players enjoy playing as famous players like Messi, Ronaldo, or Neymar. But if those players aren't available, then gamers can choose a talented player from a lesser-known club, such as Timo Werner of Red Bull Leipzig or Papu Gómez of Sevilla.

With every copy of *FIFA* sold, the game increases its record over other sports video games. So the next time you play *FIFA* you can tell your friends: We're helping to set an amazing world record!

Since 2004 *FIFA* players from around the globe have competed in the FIFA eWorld Cup. More than 2 million players sign up for the tournament each year in the hope of reaching the finals in London.

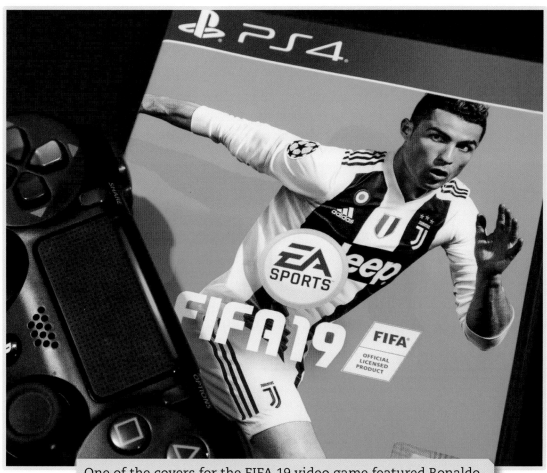

One of the covers for the FIFA 19 video game featured Ronaldo.

Best-Selling Sports Video Game Franchises

GAME	FIRST RELEASE	TOTAL COPIES SOLD
FIFA	1993	325 million
Madden NFL	1988	130 million
Pro Evolution Soccer	1995	109 million
NBA 2K	1999	90 million
Gran Turismo	1997	80 million

BIG-TIME MOMENTS IN SOCCER

1872

The Football Association Challenge Cup
is awarded for the first time in England.

1894

The first soccer match is played in Brazil.

1902

Barcelona and Real Madrid play
their first match against each other.

1930

First World Cup tournament is played
in Uruguay. The host country defeats
Argentina to win the championship.

1950

Uruguay defeats Brazil at the
Maracanã Stadium to win the World Cup.

1956

Real Madrid wins the first European Cup.
The tournament will eventually be
called the Champions League.

1958

Pelé plays in his first World Cup for Brazil.

1966

England wins its only World Cup.

1977

Pelé finishes his career playing
for the New York Cosmos.

1982
The University of North Carolina women's soccer team wins its first NCAA national championship.

1996
Major League Soccer is created in United States.

1999
Brandi Chastain scores the final goal and the U.S. Women's National Team wins the Women's World Cup.

2003
Marta scores her first goal for the Brazilian women's national team.

2004
Lionel Messi plays his first game for Barcelona.

2007
David Beckham joins the LA Galaxy.

2014
Germany defeats Argentina in most-watched soccer game ever.

2018
Cristiano Ronaldo is oldest player to score a hat trick in the World Cup.

2020
Christine Sinclair sets all-time record for most international goals.

GLOSSARY

capacity (kuh-PASS-uh-tee)—the number of people who can fit inside a stadium or arena

crest (KREST)—the logo or symbol of a soccer team, usually worn on the chest of the jersey

dynasty (DYE-nuh-stee)—a sports team that wins multiple championships over a period of several years

equalizer (EE-kwul-eye-zer)—in soccer, a goal that ties the score

exhibition (ek-suh-BI-shuhn)—a game or match played only for show, which does not count in the standings or for a tournament

hat trick (HAT TRIK)—when a player scores three goals in one game

header (HED-uhr)—a shot where players use their heads to pass or shoot the ball

hormone (HOR-mohn)—a chemical made by a gland in the body that affects a person's growth and development

penalty kick (PEN-uhl-tee KIK)—a free kick awarded to the offense when the defense commits a penalty

professional (pruh-FESH-uh-nuhl)—a person who makes money by doing something that others might do without being paid

rival (RYE-vuhl)—a person or team that is often faced in a competition

shootout (SHOOT-out)—a method of breaking a tie score at the end of a game; five players from each team take turns shooting at the opponent's goal, and the team that scores the most goals wins

tournament (TUR-nuh-muhnt)—a series of matches between several players or teams, ending in one winner

READ MORE

Bowker, Paul. *Soccer Records.* Lake Elmo, MN: Focus Readers, 2021.

Mooney, Carla. *Ronaldo vs. Messi vs. Beckham vs. Pelé.* New York: Rosen Publishing, 2020.

Stead, Emily. *Women's Soccer Superstars: Record-Breaking Players, Teams, and Tournaments!* New York: Macmillan, 2021.

INTERNET SITES

Major League Soccer
mlssoccer.com/

Pelé
britannica.com/biography/Pele-Brazilian-athlete

Sports Illustrated KIDS
sikids.com

INDEX